EMOTIONAL INTELLIGENCE
FOR KINGDOM LEADERS

a primer and 30 day journal

BRIAN BENNETT
multiplyleaders.co

Cover and Book Design by Kristin White   www.fourohseven.com
Published by MultiplyLeaders   www.multiplyleaders.co

This book is grace to me in many ways, on many levels.

Dearest Katie, your presence and quiet, steadfast love is a gift. Your support made this possible.

Joel and Jedd, may you think and feel deeply. May God's glory always be the aim of your lives. May you always be confident that your dad loves you and believes in you deeply. You bring dad great joy.

Thanks to Larry Bennett Jr. for his invaluable feedback on the manuscript and for his support that made this work possible. You are a man of generosity, encouragement, loyalty and love.

Thanks to Rick Reichert for his very helpful feedback and work as well on the manuscript. He has been an ongoing encouragement to me.

Heartfelt appreciation to Bret for being a listener in the dark nights of my soul, in the most vulnerable moments. Your patience was a gift.

I count it the deepest of privileges to serve alongside the extraordinary ministry leaders of Calvary Church, both staff and volunteers. What a gift it is to serve beside such loving and gifted people.

To my parents who were first generation Christians, thank you for carving out the path you've passed on to me. I thank God for your courage.

Thanks to Chad Myers for his insight and feedback that made this work better.

CONTENTS

Character is grown to the degree that we love God and others. Love that is true and eternal begins with worship of the God who redeems people by his unexpected and unreasonable grace. We grow in character, then, to the degree we are captured by gratitude and awe.

Dan Allender, Leading with a Limp

INTRODUCTION

This isn't an exhaustive overview, but rather a primer on emotional intelligence for kingdom leaders in the home, workplace and church. It is an introduction that I hope will whet your appetite for further pursuit. It is also a framework for cultivating awareness, self-reflection and emotionally healthy disciplines.

I approach this as a fellow traveler on the journey, sharing out of my own failures, learnings and experiences. The challenge found in growing in our emotional intelligence is that we are forever on a continuing journey this side of God's full restoration.

The heart is a tricky thing, and the effects of sin upon it have led us into a brokenness that not only results in separation from God and each other, but also a separation within our own selves. We no longer experience an inner congruence and harmonious experience. It is far too easy to betray ourselves, to live from shame instead of grace, and to posture something better instead of giving the world our true self. We are all on a journey of growth and transformation, a journey that takes many twists and turns, a journey that requires us both to contribute and to be led.

So, from this place of caring deeply for kingdom leaders and seeing the enormous value of applying emotional intelligence in my own journey (that I continue today), I write to you. Consider this an invitation wherever you are on the path. If you are at the beginning of this journey then perhaps the pages ahead will push you uncomfortably to new places of awareness and cause you to question how far you are willing to trust yourself with God. For others, who are farther into this journey, please hold old questions and paradigms with fresh hands. God is ever speaking and guiding us further into dependent life with him. Realize that new knowledge is important, but deeper application of old knowledge may be even more significant to our growth.

Awareness and instruction on emotional health and intelligence in the church is growing and picking up steam, yet there is far more progress to be made. It is an area that has been neglected in leadership preparation, teaching and the life of the church, but it is a gold mine of growth for those willing to live out their emotional life under the reign and grace of King Jesus. Emotional health is essential to experiencing the freedom and light yoke that Jesus calls us to in the Gospels.

As you work through this journal, may God meet you where you are each day, may He quiet you with His radical love and grace, and may He trigger paradigm shifts in your thinking that enable you to know a fuller experience of resurrection life.

START HERE

The first part of the book is a short primer of core content and key principles that will help you unlock and fuel emotionally intelligent living. The rest of the book is a 30 day journal to guide readers in engagement and experience. Read the primer before you start journaling. After reading the primer, begin the journaling process until you have completed the 30 day reflection process. Working multiple days at once defeats the purpose. The exercise is as much about cultivating an internal presence of emotional health and vitality by practicing reflection each day, as it is about the actual journaling content. Don't short-change the process. Don't rush. That is a sign of emotional unhealthiness. Breathe. Relax. Live deeply. Don't worry if you miss a day. It may take you two months to complete. Stick with it. Try to pick a time and a place each day when you will reflect. Schedule it into your calendar. Some may want to do it in the morning, others in the evening. Others may look to build in margin to reflect at morning, midday and evening. For others, slowing down before the end of the day and reflecting back over the events experienced will be a tremendous first step. What will help you continue to thrive? Remember, the quality of the reflection and our willingness to let ourselves be present in the moment is essential to real movement, otherwise it will just be another exercise, another 'to do' on our list.

Feel free to skip questions, but don't hide from any. Skip ones that are unnecessary to you, but don't skip questions because they feel too hard, make you feel vulnerable or are too probing. Those are the especially powerful ones that will unlock the doors of growth as we enter into them in God's grace. The point isn't to just get the journal done. The goal is to go on an inward journey with ourselves and the Lord that in turn benefits others as well.

One final note. At the end of each day's reflection, there is a place to write out a prayer. I can't encourage you strongly enough to speak to the Lord about your emotions. If we are not opening up this aspect of ourselves to the Lord, we will ultimately stunt our growth. David models a beautiful engagement of honesty with the Lord emotionally in the Psalms. Let's follow his lead.

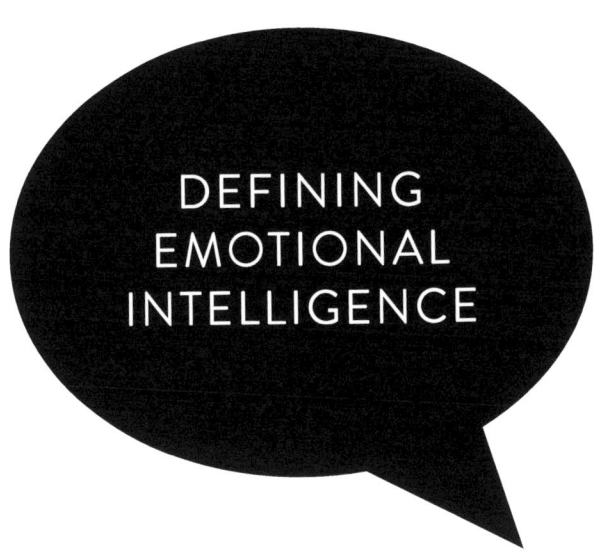

DEFINING EMOTIONAL INTELLIGENCE

Are your emotions holding you back or propelling you forward? Whether we recognize it or not, our emotions are influencing every conversation, relationship, challenge and opportunity we experience. In these crucial moments of our lives, our interactions with our own emotions and those of others is either empowering or hindering the dreams, purposes and values that are planted deep in our hearts.

Miles can't seem to hold a job for very long. Every few years "it doesn't work out." He is angry and resentful, feeling defeated as he sits at home and looks online to find new opportunities. Deep down he doesn't believe the world is being fair to him. He is a victim. But if you asked his previous co-workers, you would hear the same story over and over. "Miles only sees things from his perspective." "He doesn't work well with others." "When under stress, he can implode." "He seems either really high or really low, you never know who is going to walk into the office." "He is unreliable." But Miles can't hear it. There is always someone else to point the finger at, someone out to get him at each new opportunity.

If he could only look in the mirror, admit his faults and take responsibility, things could begin to change for him.

Will and Lauren's marriage is on the rocks. There were times where it seemed to be in a better place, but the weight of children and financial challenges is pressing on them. They are cracking under the pressure. Using coping strategies they've learned from their childhood, their fights escalate and escalate until they don't talk for days. Their emotional bank accounts with each other are dangerously low. Will doesn't realize his own insecurities about providing for his family are driving his patterns of attacking in their conflicts. Lauren thinks it's all Will's fault, she can't see how the disrespect she shows Will over their financial struggles is driven by an unhealthy need to control everything. They need to become aware of what is driving their behaviors under the surface and better process their perspectives if they are going to make it.

Beth is the new ministry leader at Willard Grove Community Church. She is gifted and passionate, and she is failing. Her first year there has been a disaster. She came in with big vision and a readiness to make the changes that were needed to help the church connect with the younger generation. She is in constant conflict and has had repeated conversations with the senior pastor about slowing down with the changes. She is starting to feel trapped. She doesn't know it, but the elders are beginning to ask the lead pastor if she really is the right person for the role. She needs to learn that relational trust is essential to leadership. If she will last another year there, she must also learn how to lead change effectively, being able to empathize and see from the perspective of others.

Jim has a track record as an effective leader, but he is stuck. Everyone can see it, but him. He has forgotten some of the most basic lessons of leadership he learned along the way. His talk and his actions don't line up. His team is growing tired of his leadership and he is blind to his influence eroding. He needs the feedback of his peers and direct reports, but he has created a culture around himself that is impenetrable. No one feels safe to get through his defenses. He keeps those who could help him most at arm's length. If something doesn't change, the bubble he has created around himself will cave soon.

These case studies reveal the need for growing our emotional intelligence if we will be leaders who last in the home, workplace and community. Growth in emotional intelligence will help each character in the stories above grow towards their full potential in Jesus. The question is, will they lean in and trust His grace and power so that God can do a deep work in their lives? The same question is true for each of us. As we explore the definition and unpack the core concepts of emotional intelligence, we must be ready to go on a journey of transformation.

Simply defining Emotional Intelligence (EI) can be challenging as there are numerous definitions that emphasize different aspects or schools of thought. I chose this definition from **Emotional Intelligence 2.0** because it is simple, memorable and holistic. "Emotional intelligence is your ability to recognize and understand emotions in yourself and others, and your ability to use this awareness to manage your behavior and relationships."[1]

The first thing that we need to be clear about is that emotional intelligence can be developed because it is an ability. It may be very challenging, depending on our life story and experiences, but nonetheless, EI can be cultivated and shaped. When we state it is an ability or competency, this means it is a skill to be learned with a potential to blossom.

There are three key skills described in the definition: recognizing, understanding and managing. *Recognizing* refers to our ability to be aware of what we are experiencing. Richard Lane describes 5 levels of awareness. As I overview them, try to identify where you typically experience emotions: "The five levels of emotional awareness in ascending order are (5) physical sensations, (4) action tendencies, (3) single emotions, (2) blends of emotions, and (1) blends of blends of emotional experience (the capacity to appreciate complexity in the experiences of the self and others)." [2]

Our physiology registers our emotions quicker than our internal awareness. As we become more skilled we move from only physical outer awareness to include our inner awareness as well. Recognition or conscious awareness, is the beginning of emotional intelligence.

Understanding moves us from simply recognizing our experience to forming meaning and gaining insight. Now that we've become aware of our anger or sadness, we are able to also unpack why we feel what we are feeling. Understanding means we must interpret the story we've told ourselves surrounding an event, relationship or situation that has led us to the feelings we are experiencing. In the New York Times bestseller, *Crucial Conversations*, the authors note that we must pay close attention to the stories we tell that attach meaning to our experiences.

"As it turns out, there is an intermediate step between what others do and how we feel. Just after we observe what others do and just before we feel some emotion about it, we tell ourselves a story. We add meaning to the action we've observed. We make a guess at the motive driving their behavior." [3]

Many times we move from feeling to acting without any awareness of the story we've told ourselves that gave meaning to the interaction or event that triggered strong emotions. Our first step is recognizing the emotion exists, then as we allow ourselves to feel it and experience it, we unpack the story we associate with it. This is uncomfortable for some of us who have grown up in churches or home environments where we didn't see feelings expressed, or we saw feelings constantly out of control. It is also uncomfortable if we were shaped by environments that taught us to be so suspicious of emotions that they simply didn't have a role in our humanity. We gain emotional intelligence by first allowing ourselves to feel and then seeking to understand these feelings. If we do not process emotions in a healthy manner, we can be aware, but make little progress on our emotional journeys.

Pastor and author of *Emotionally Healthy Spirituality* Peter Scazzero drives the significance of this point home when he calls us to "Allow yourself to experience the full weight of your feelings. Allow them without censoring them. Then you can reflect and thoughtfully decide what to do with them." [4]

That leads us to the final action, *managing* our responses. When we are unaware or do not seek to understand our emotional signals, we can move too quickly to reacting in a way that doesn't align with our values and causes harm to ourselves or others. From speaking too sharply to a spouse or co-worker, to not managing the nerves we feel before a presentation. The three skills of recognizing, understanding and managing empower us to overcome limiting perspectives, attitudes, and behaviors. If we are not managing our responses then we are being driven by deep emotions that are flying under the radar. This may seem fine when we are having a great day and the sun is shining brightly in the blue sky, but this can become very problematic when stress from work triggers unbalanced discipline of a child. There are times as a parent that my son may be having a meltdown, but my reaction might say more about my internal state than his current misbehavior. When we let hurt build up over time into bitter resentment, we inevitably allow toxic emotions to leak out of us as slander, gossip or negativity. Managing our responses is more than limiting unhealthy reactions, it is also essential to our motivation, focus and adaptability.

Notice the breadth of the definition given. It is recognizing, understanding and managing emotions in *ourselves* and in relationship with *others*. Our ability to recognize our own emotions and our ability to detect what a friend or colleague is experiencing are both essential skills for of EI. These personal and social awareness skills are fundamental to succeeding in relationships, leading teams and being a person of influence or credibility.

Below are three examples that highlight the three core actions of EI in motion.

Example 1 | A Lack of Recognition

Tim gets cut off as he is driving from his house, running late to work. He can't believe that guy didn't even signal and cut it that close. Tim tailgates the man for the next four blocks, until he hears sirens behind him and realizes he is getting pulled over. Now, he's not only late for work, but will be paying a fine. His day is going from bad to worse.

Example 2 | Awareness but a Lack of Understanding and Managing His Response

Tim feels angry as he walks out of the door after an abrupt conversation with his wife. He feels the tension inside as he slams the door and looks at his watch, realizing the conversation put him a few minutes behind. As he is replaying the conversation over and over in his head on his way to work, some guy cuts him off. He feels furious. He is so angry that he would love to get close enough to tell this guy off. He tailgates him for the next four blocks until he hears sirens behind him. Now, he's not only late for work, but will be paying a fine. He realizes he lost his temper as the officer walks up and asks him if he knew how close he was to the car in front of him.

Example 3 | Recognizing, Understanding and Managing a Healthy Response

Tim feels angry as he walks out of the door after an abrupt conversation with his wife. As he walks to his car, he recognizes that he is feeling strongly. In the back of his mind, he acknowledges that he might have been quick to speak harshly to his wife in the kitchen. He has felt a high level of stress at work lately finishing a big project and feels like he might be bringing it home. He thinks about how he could have handled the conversation differently, how he could of just verbalized the stress he is feeling and asked her to have the conversation about dinner with the new neighbor later that night. As he is contemplating his feelings and responses, the car next to him cuts him off, cutting it close enough that Tim feels a sudden burst of anger. "Why do people drive like this?" Part of him wants to give this guy a piece of his mind, but he knows he is still riding strong on the emotions he felt coming out the door. He acknowledges he feels anxious and on high alert. He starts honestly praying out loud about his actions and feelings as he continues to drive to work. He seeks to relax and make the best out of the day ahead after a rough start.

Which example above typically describes your level of awareness, understanding and response to your daily life?

As you look at each example, what level of awareness is Tim functioning at? What would have been a next step for him in each example?

To make this definition stick, let's put it into action and start plumbing the current level of our own emotional intelligence. Take a moment to think back over your day so far. Walk through each aspect of the definition and make notes. If you are struggling to answer the questions, let your day play like a movie in your head where you are watching yourself and try to remember what you were feeling. See if you can distinguish thinking and feeling in those moments. Use the questions below to guide you.

What emotions did you experience?

Why might you have felt that way?

What story did you tell yourself in those experiences that led you to those emotions?

How did you respond?

How consciously aware were you of your emotions when you were responding?

Looking back, would you have changed anything about your response?

What did you learn about yourself and your emotional intelligence from this time of reflection?

How consciously aware were you of your emotions when you were responding?

Looking back, would you have changed anything about your response?

What did you learn about yourself and your emotional intelligence from this time of reflection?

Where are you strongest? Recognizing, understanding or managing?

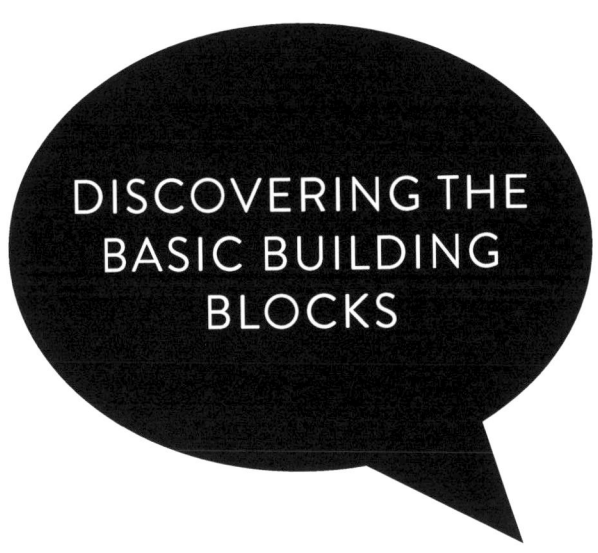

DISCOVERING THE
BASIC BUILDING
BLOCKS

Now that we've explored what emotional intelligence (EI) is, we can dive deeper into the four core components that are at the heart of EI. These core four build off each other consecutively. They are found in multiple readings, but I first discovered them in *Emotional Intelligence 2.0*, through taking an EI assessment. It is very likely that each of us is stronger in two and weaker in two of the components. EI is active and dynamic, so in a sense we never arrive. By understanding these core competencies, it empowers us to discover and develop strategies that will help us thrive.

01 Self-Awareness

"When we hide from what we feel—from emotion—we hide from the truth."[5] Accurate 'Self-Awareness' is the building block for every aspect of EI. Self-awareness means we are perceptive of our behaviors, attitudes, beliefs, values and emotions. We have a pulse on who we are and how we are experiencing the world. Dr. David Walton describes self-awareness as:

"Knowing your own strengths, weaknesses and limitations, being open to what is happening around you, valuing feedback, having a sense of humor and perspective, the capacity to reflect and to learn from experience, being open to change."[6]

It is far too easy to live with low self-awareness where we are either unaware of what we are feeling or only aware in a surface manner that doesn't really help us. When we live unaware, we are driven by emotional responses we do not even know exist. I remember a recent incident where I was unaware as I came home from a long day at work and had a deep sense of tiredness and loneliness from pouring into others. I was feeling empty. I arrived with deep emotional needs, but wasn't aware of how they were driving me. I expected my wife to meet those needs without even a hint of awareness that during this same time she had been at home all day with our two young children who had demanded much attention and energy from her. I was so driven by under the surface needs that I didn't empathize with her at all, but simply walked in the door and expected her to fill my emotional cup. This is all happening at a very low level of consciousness, as I was simply seeing from my first person perspective. The results weren't good. My wife needed a few moments to herself having just put the children to bed. If I had let myself become more aware of my inner emotional state I could have acknowledged my deep desire for connection, but I also would have been able to better empathize with her.

In leadership and relationships, our lack of self-awareness leads to a lack of effective communication. This results in failure of relationships and unnecessary relational hurt. Daniel Goleman helps us think about this when he says, "Thus there are two levels of emotion, conscious and unconscious. The moment an emotion comes into awareness marks its registering as such in the frontal cortex."[7] Recently we went for our son's checkup at the hospital after a very trying medical journey over the past year. I knew I had felt various emotions over that season from sadness to hope, but I didn't realize there were strong emotions present just under the surface that came out as we walked through the doors into the lobby. I felt unexpected tears in my eyes, a mix of joy and sadness over the journey we had experienced. I was surprised by these emotions. If you would have asked me what words described my emotions that day, I probably wouldn't have known them. Perhaps, I was unaware because I was tired of feeling those emotions. Perhaps, I was unaware because I was too busy. Whenever we are surprised by emotions, it normally means we haven't been very aware of them. Awareness is an intentional discipline that helps us move from a life of unconsciousness to conscious experience, from sleep walking to life in color. This shift from emotional unawareness to awareness is essential to growth and success, both personally and relationally. This is why we must cultivate a greater, non-judgmental understanding of ourselves, becoming especially in tune to our inner signals.[8] As we learn to tune into our own joy, sadness, pain and values, we can then live with a greater experience of congruence and wholeness. Being aware is not the same as being imprisoned by our emotional impulses or experiences. "Self-awareness is not an attention that gets carried away by emotions, overreacting and amplifying what is perceived. Rather, it is a neutral mode that maintains self-reflectiveness even amidst turbulent emotions."[9] Awareness is an ability to acknowledge and allow ourselves to experience whatever emotion we are feeling instead of suppressing, ignoring or denying it. This is only possible when we do not rush to judgment about our emotions, but instead, simply recognize our emotional state.

In order to cultivate this awareness, we need to grow towards the fullness of our redeemed humanity in Christ. We must learn to live out of grace. Grace frees us to look honestly in the mirror and see everything that is really there. It calls us out of hiding. Grace also makes it safe for us to discover our story, the good, the bad and the ugly. Knowing that nothing separates us from the Father's love in Christ, we are freed to live honestly with ourselves and others. Our ability to see ourselves as we truly are, to plumb the depth of our own personhood, and to bring the subconscious into the conscious, is directly proportionate to our trust and application of the lavish grace of God. This is not an easy application, but a freeing one as we learn to press into unconditional acceptance. For there we discover who we truly are in relationship to Him.

02 Self-Management

'Self-Management' is the second core competency of EI, which builds off self-awareness. "Without recognizing our own emotions, we will be poor at managing them, and less able to understand them in others." [10] We cannot manage or respond purposefully to our emotional experiences until they first register in our consciousness, but this doesn't mean our body isn't experiencing the weight of unconscious feelings. That is why we might blow up on a co-worker or spouse and find ourselves surprised at our level of intensity. We can be unaware of how our emotions built up over time towards them or how an experience completely unrelated earlier in the day has stuck with us. [11] When this happens those emotions begin to leak into our behavior. "To manage our emotions, we need to be able to take control of our behaviors; to do that, we must first be able to recognize them." [12]

'Self-Management' is the ability to integrate our emotions into our lives in a healthy manner consistent with our values. This competency recognizes that we can choose our responses to our emotions and that we are not captivated to follow their every whim. Self-management combines self-awareness and self-understanding into healthy actions. Instead of withdrawing from a hard conversation, we are able to overcome avoiding the conflict and head into it with humility and confidence to share our story and handle the awkwardness. As I think back on various challenging conversations over the years as a leader, I can clearly see ones that I didn't handle well or avoided altogether because I felt such strong anxiety internally and didn't know how to manage it. I can be a 'people pleaser' if I am not aware. If I don't acknowledge that personal reality and root myself in God's value of me instead of someone else's, I can be crippled by fear. For others, the opposite is true. We don't shy away but have a tendency to explode. Or we might shy away at first and then let things build up till we overreact to something that isn't the real issue.

Tina's Story | Overcoming Anxiety

With Tina's new promotion, additional new skills needed to be learned. She was excited as she walked back to her office after meeting with her boss. However, she barely had time for the news to soak in before fear started to creep into her awareness. Because of her new role, her boss asked her to prepare and give a presentation to the executives from headquarters who were in town next Monday. She ignored her para-lyzing fear of public speaking for a moment as her friend Susan stopped by. Over the coming week, she was so busy engaged in meetings with her new team members that she barely had time to think, let alone prepare for Monday's presentation. On Saturday morning, she woke up with a deep heaviness and dread. She was mentally exhausted and emotionally depleted. The constant interactions with her former team members stopping in to congratulate her and the introductions to new team members left her with little time to herself. Suddenly thoughts of inadequacy started filling her mind. What if I fail? Who am I to give this presentation? I am not good at public speaking. What if they think they made a mistake? What if I forget what I prepared? She brewed a fresh cup of coffee and headed to the back porch to think. As she re-flected she realized she was letting her mind become focused on failure. She realized in this moment that she didn't have a strong sense of her self-value outside her job performance. She took time to slow down and remind herself that her significance comes from Jesus. Driving in to work on Monday, there were butterflies. She had battled them all week-end. But the difference now was her self-talk was rooted not in failure, but in God's grace and presence with her. She acknowledge that failure was possible, but it wasn't final. She also reminded herself of times in the past when she had done well in public speaking despite her nerves. She thanked God for her recent promotion and breathed deeply for a few minutes in her car. The anxiety wasn't completely gone, but she was ready to go.

Good self-management also improves our ability to take the mantle of greater responsibilities and not be engulfed by them. It helps us effectively assess and navigate opportunities and challenges. When our area of responsibility doubles, instead of becoming overwhelmed and failing to meet the new challenge, we move forward with a calm resilience in the uncertainty. It is both a limiting and expanding competency. Self-management means we limit or don't act on negative impulses that are inconsistent with our values. For example, we feel lonely and an affair looks tempting but we don't act on it. We feel stressed about money challenges and we have an opportunity to embezzle but we don't. Someone else receives a promotion that we think we were more qualified for and in conversation we can undermine their recently received authority with other co-workers but choose not to. When we choose not to act in these situations, while having an internal desire to do so, we are applying our EI under the leadership of Jesus.

Positively, EI also relates to our motivation. As with anything worth doing, at some point we will grow tired and weary of the mission we set out to accomplish. Self-management abilities enable us to persevere, act on self-care, reflect on visions of the future that inspire us and overcome challenges. High EI in this core competency keeps us from quitting early, enables us to stay focused, and helps us continue to make progress. As kingdom leaders, we recognize that we are incapable of living and making changes on our own. Emotional intelligence clarifies some of the challenges and opportunities as it relates to our growth, enabling us to apply these principles by the grace of Jesus and the power of the Holy Spirit. We don't seek to change in our strength, but instead live with a posture of surrendered openness before the Lord. Knowing how our emotional life influences our every action gives us helpful paradigms for living an integrated life, but it doesn't diminish our need for utter dependence upon the Lord. We never outgrow our need of abiding in Him. We just learn to include our emotional life in our abiding.

03 Social-Awareness

Just as 'Self-Awareness' is a recognition of our own emotions, beliefs, attitudes and values, so 'Social-Awareness' is a recognition and understanding of what others are feeling and experiencing. People who are high in social-awareness can read the emotions of a group gathered at a staff meeting. They can sense in the tone, body language and responses of a friend when something is wrong or perhaps very right. With friends who are close to me, I can usually look them in the eye and get a quick feeling of where they are at. There are many other signals to watch for as well. We can always pick up on someone's nervous tapping of their feet, eyes wandering distractedly away from the conversation, slumped posture, quick speech or a strong sense of excitement. "The key to intuiting another's feelings is the ability to read nonverbal channels: the tone of voice, gesture, facial expression, and the like." [13] Sometimes I have found myself in conversation with another person and they've asked me if I am 'alright' to my surprise. "Absolutely," I respond, "I am doing well." Only later, when another person asked me the same question or, in a quiet moment, did I realize that I felt overwhelmed or under pressure. These people had detected something. My lack of awareness in that moment kept me from recognizing my true emotions, but my body language communicated something else. People who have cultivated 'Social-Awareness' are not only able to read body language, they can hear the emotional meaning behind the words, understanding what the person may be feeling.

"Effective communication comes down to listening and speaking with your heart. When people feel understood emotionally, they feel cared for. This is very different from listening to someone from the head—that is, looking merely for the content of the person's words, without paying attention to the emotion. The goal of effective communication is to understand the emotional message of the speaker. You have to ask yourself, what is this person feeling?" [14]

Many times when I am in a pastoral counseling session with someone, I have my best listening antenna up. I am fully present, absorbing every signal the other person is sending me. And as I am fully present in those moments, I can feel the significance of a story that the person sharing might not even be aware of. Or I may sense the pain behind a statement they just said and it surprises them when tears come quickly as I call attention to it for further exploration. The challenge for me is to live with that kind of awareness in other environments. Preparing for a counseling session causes me to mentally prepare and get ready to be a great listener. In the hustle and bustle of normal life, I find it easy to not listen with the same attentiveness and care. We make significant progress when we are able to not only repeat what our spouse or coworker just said to us, but connect with the emotion from which they said it. Then we can explore the meaning in their words and emotions.

Sarah's Example

Sarah was deeply frustrated with her husband ever since they left the hometown they both grew up in when he accepted a call to take his first senior pastorate of a church three states away. She felt constantly angry with him, even over the most minor things. He was gone all the time and she started to think he really didn't care about her anymore. Finally, one night after dinner, as he went to open his laptop in the study, everything came to a head. "You're never home and I hate it here," she cried. "This church isn't welcoming and I will never fit in. You care more about this church than you do about me." Her husband was shocked. At first, he was frustrated because he felt overwhelmed trying hard to succeed in his new role. Quickly though, in that moment as Sarah cried, he realized he hadn't been in tune with her and she had a point in what she was saying. He had been so busy at church getting settled and trying to keep up with his new responsibilities that he didn't have a clue she was feeling this deeply. If he is listening closely, he will hear not just that she wants him home more, that is likely true, but also that she feels lonely, afraid, and insecure in this new place. As he listens to her explore these emotions, he might likely find that she is really mourning the loss as well of her family relationships she left behind. If he is practicing high EI, he will acknowledge not only the changes he needs to make, but also listen to her heart and let her explore those emotions without trying to rush towards fixing them. He will just be with her.

Social-awareness includes the ability to empathize or experience and understand the perspective of another. "That capacity — the ability to know how another feels comes into play in a vast array of life arenas, from sales and management to romance and parenting, to compassion and political action." [15] As we study these core competencies, it becomes clear very quickly how these relate to every aspect of our lives. To grow in social-awareness, we must grow first in our own self-awareness, and then in our abilities to observe others and listen deeply to them. We observe their body language, posture, eye contact, and level of anxiousness. We listen to their tone, pacing, volume and what their voice communicates about their values and energy. In every interaction with another, we experience their emotional presence and they experience ours. Our internal systems naturally will sync up if we are paying attention and present with them. We will understand their feelings, hear their heart behind their words and read between the lines. But first we must be present and aware, observing and listening, receiving and sending signals that make for a strong connection.

04 Relationship-Management

'Relationship-Management' combines social-awareness with purposeful responses that align values and health to foster thriving connections with others. Regardless of a person's personality or temperament, those strong in this core competency can relate well with others, appreciating differences and are good at navigating group dynamics. If we are weak in this area, we will struggle by continuing to practice the emotional coping responses we learned through our childhood. "In other words, the way people learn to manage emotional states as children will follow them into their adult friendships, marriages, and work relationships."[16] Developing strong relational-management abilities requires the previous three competencies and a willingness to explore the past's effect on the present. The more purposeful and skillful we become in activating self-awareness, self-management, and social-awareness, the more we will be able to combine them into healthy relationships at home, work and in our church communities.

Cultivating our relationship-management skills enables us to authentically and genuinely engage in meaningful relationships. This does not mean conflict free relationships. It does mean that we are willing to give ourselves and receive others in ways that encourage healthy friendships and connections. Practicing EI means growing more comfortable in our own skin, accepting who we are as image bearers in God's grace, and receiving His affirmation of us in Christ. This leads us into authentically healthy encounters. "Authenticity is the permission we give ourselves to be who we really are...It frees us to communicate openly without concerns about not being recognized, understood, accepted for who we are, or being invisible or overshadowed by others." [17] Embracing our identity from Jesus, and letting him define our significance and value, enables us to live differentiated from others. This means that we are rooted and secure enough in who we are, that we care about others, but aren't imprisoned by their opinions and approval. We can be together with others without losing ourselves in the process. We are able to be in relationships, but have a strong and well defined sense of self. We know who we are and are able to not over or under function with our families, friends or spouse. In difficult conversations, we can understand the viewpoint of others and still hold a differing position. Differentiation is significant to mature relationships because it means we are not only secure in ourselves, but also are able to appreciate the uniqueness and gift of various temperaments, experiences and perspectives in other people. It also helps us to extend grace to one another, freeing us from trying to remake others in our image, demanding perfection from others, or hiding from our own vulnerability. Instead, as detailed in the excellent book *Crucial Conversations*, we can develop the skills to create safety for different shared pools of meaning, challenging perspectives and conflict resolution.[18] Strengthening our relational management empowers us to know others and be known in healthy relationships, with the skills and paradigms to cultivate meaningful interactions. This EI competency is central to the way we love others and act towards them in Jesus' name. As we watch Jesus in the gospels interacting with various people from different backgrounds, we see this competency modeled beautifully. Jesus doesn't honor every expectation placed on him by others, while still living as a Servant-King. He was able to withstand verbal attacks by religious leaders and hold his ground. He was able to cross social and political boundaries in moments like His encounter with the woman at the well in John 4. He knew who He was and why He was sent. This empowered and enabled His ministry. His responses, in all his interactions, were filled with grace and truth.

Kevin's Example | Dealing with Hurt

Kevin was so angry that he was talking out loud to himself as he walked from the office to his car. "I can't believe he did that," he thought. "How many times has Ryan shared something confidential that I opened up to him about?" "This is the last time," he said as he climbed into his truck. He sat there for a minute looking out of the windshield and just thinking. Ryan and Kevin had been friends for a longtime. They knew everything about each other and had a deep friendship. But sometimes, Ryan would let stuff slip. In the past Kevin got angry but didn't know how to deal with it without losing the friendship, so he just tried to let it go. "I can't trust him," Kevin said to himself almost without thinking. Earlier today a coworker walked up to Kevin in the hallway and said, "I want you to know I am praying for you and your marriage." Kevin felt confused and betrayed right away. "How did they know that my marriage was struggling?" I've only shared that with Ryan and I told him it was between us. Kevin felt like just giving up on the relationship. He didn't trust Ryan after the latest breach. But as he pulled into his own driveway after a long commute home, he knew the he had to bring it up to Ryan and let him know this had broken his trust. He didn't know what the relationship would look like after that, but he knew he owed it to himself and to Ryan, after years of deep friendship, to be honest about the hurt.

Kara's Example | Seeking Courage and Health

Kara was the newest staff member at her church and was charged with leading the worship ministry. One of her peers, Mark, was making life difficult. He was loud, pushy and didn't care about anyone else's opinion. He had been there for a few years longer than her and no one seemed to know how to respond to his rudeness or intimidation in meetings. His ideas tended to be accepted and implemented, regardless if they were the best for the church or not, because no one felt safe challenging him. Kara was starting to regret taking the job and ministering in a work environment that seemed to be so full of stress and unhealthiness. She would hear people in the hallway after some of the meetings and, at times, people even came by her office asking if she could believe how Mark acted. But no one would actually talk to Mark. Kara knew things couldn't go on as they were. She could just quietly leave or she could go through the hard work of helping create a different work environment. She didn't know if she would make it through the process without getting let go herself. It felt very unsafe to upset the apple cart, regardless of how dysfunctional it was. No matter what happened, her job didn't define her value, she reminded herself as she walked into Mark's office. She asked him if he had a minute. She decided to have a grace and truth conversation with Mark, and if he didn't receive it, she had determined to go the senior pastor with her concerns. It would have been easier to just leave, but she wanted what was best not only for her and the church, but also for Mark. No matter how hard this was for her, this gave him an opportunity to choose health.

Larry and Linda's Example | Cultivating Deepening Intimacy in Marriage

Larry and Linda had been married for more than 30 years. They had their rough patches like any other couple, but had found ways of evolving through those seasons and working through their struggles in a way that led to a rich love for one another and deep friendship in their marriage. When asked recently in their class at church what the secret was to a long and fulfilling marriage, Larry responded that they always tried to love each other as Christ had loved them. That meant paying attention to the needs of each other, listening to the meaning behind the words, apologizing and owning their failures when they were wrong. It also meant affirming one another's temperament and gift differences. Linda chimed in that paying attention to each other's unique love languages was essential to making emotional deposits into the other person's bank account. "There were times," Linda continued, "where we felt at a loss for moving the relationship forward, overcoming a season of hurt. But we kept facing one another, we kept listening and seeking to love." "Communication was huge in every season," Larry said as he jumped back in. "When we first were married, I had no idea how to really communicate in a deep way that helped us connect. I didn't come from a family where people shared their emotions and experiences like that. It took me awhile to figure it out. Really, I grew in communication as we went to counseling after one particularly rough patch, that's how I learned to connect with Linda by not only giving her my mind, but also my heart. Over the years we've learned to make it safe to talk about anything, and not let things build up. We don't do it perfect, but we're getting better and better."

Mike's Example | Leading His Team Towards Greater Effectiveness

When Mike took over the lead role at an established missionary agency, he had no idea how unhealthy the culture was. It was toxic. Very quickly, his enthusiasm turned into a sense of dread as he drove into the office each day. The staff meetings were lifeless. Fear and distrust seemed thick enough in the room to cut with a knife. People were friendly and cordial on the outside, but years of unhealth had built up. The staff wasn't motivated around their mission and it showed. Mike knew he had been brought in to help turn things around. The board had talked about that, but they didn't reveal how desperate the team climate really was. The former leader had led with a volatile and ego centered style that was abrasive and driven. The team eventually stopped believing in the mission and just started coping. They had been in this toxic 'water' for so long, they weren't even aware of how deeply it had influenced them. Mike felt overwhelmed and called his friend Dan to process his experience. Dan listened well and asked good questions. The longer they talked the more clarity Mike got as he just poured out everything he was feeling. "What are you going to do?" Dan asked as they were about to hang up. Mike didn't hesitate, "I am going to schedule an offsite day once a month for the next quarter to focus on building relationships and trust." At the first offsite, Mike could feel his disappointment as the tension followed them from the office to a local retreat center. The day started rough, but soon after some icebreaker exercises and team building, Mike thought he could feel something different in the air. For the next week afterwards things seemed much the same, but there were signs that something was also different. People still approached meetings like they had before and whatever energy they gathered from the offsite seemed to leak away, but they also talked about the shared memories from the ropes course exercise with gratitude. At the next offsite the team came more ready to share, connect and play together. It was at the third meeting that Mike saw the real breakthrough. It was the beginning, and it was the right beginning. He had the team share their personal life stories in five minutes. The tears, vulnerability, affirmation and learning was so rich. People walked away from this meeting feeling far safer with each other. Over the next year and half the culture of the team slowly turned around.

FIVE CHALLENGES

As I reflect on my life and leadership, I am going to share five challenges I struggle with as I seek to be an emotionally intelligent leader. As you read mine, think about your five.

01 Living Without Limits

I have a high capacity for getting things done. Like any strength though, there is a weakness attached to its overuse. When I am not living and leading with a healthy internal emotional state, my strength for having a high capacity moves into a self-destruction path of living without limits. This leads to burnout, resentment, exhaustion and a whole host of other challenges. I was a 'ministryholic' for the first five years of pastoring and can easily open that door if I am not careful. Thankfully, I eventually ran into a season of depression that forced me to look inward and also look outward for help. Counseling was such a grace to me as I explored and peeled back layers. No matter how many layers we've pulled back, we are never done this side of God's final restoration.

02 Withdrawing From Conflict

When we aren't secure in our Jesus identity, we aren't differentiated enough to have conflict. This is another area that I have struggled with over the years of leading. I would spiritualize or rationalize issues, overlooking them instead of having the hard conversation in a gracious manner. This hurt me and those I led. When we spiritualize conflict or rationalize it away, we don't grow into our fullness. We carry emotions internally that aren't fair to those they are aimed at. These emotions become toxic. Expressing our hurt and frustrations in a gentle way helps us live healthy instead of carrying unnecessary baggage until it boils over. It hurt my teams that I led, since a lack of conflict and effective conflict resolution ultimately hurts the mission. The best ideas simply don't come up in a conflict free zone, and we under-function because we've learned to play it too safe in our dialogues. Unhealthy personalities on the team go unchecked and eventually this demotivates and brings the whole team downward. I thought I was practicing love by not dealing directly with issues, but really the most loving thing to do is to help people grow by living honestly with them in God's grace.

03 Minimizing Relationships For The Mission

Some people are task focused, others are relationship focused. People constantly identify me as someone who loves others and, it is true, I really love people. But I also have sacrificed personal friendships for the sake of the mission. I can become so tasked focused that I love others well who are related to the ministry teams and interactions, but fail to love those well who are unrelated to the mission. This has cost me loneliness and discouragement at different seasons. I finally realized this when I saw I had many people who I loved and cared for deeply related to ministry, but too few personal friendships unrelated to the ministry. God created us for community. It is easy as a kingdom leader to make an idol out of ministry. If you read this and rationalize that relationships are just simply a cost of being mission focused, you've made an idol out of ministry and leadership like I did.

04 Suppressing Uncomfortable Emotions

As I've studied emotional intelligence, an interesting concept is the idea that we experience emotions at a conscious and subconscious level. Not earth shattering when you think about it, but when you apply it to your life and leadership, this can be a catalyst for significant growth. What emotions is your body feeling that aren't registering in your conscious- ness because we are unwilling to face them or living too fast to feel them? That might be a game changer for some of us. It is for me. I realized over the years that I tend to have faint awareness of emotions I am uncomfortable with or related to situations I am afraid to explore because of the lack of courage to deal with them effectively. I can sup- press emotions I am embarrassed or afraid of and the result is unhealthy living. The dangerous thing is I can function outwardly seemingly fine while I am internally suppressing emotions that God desires to grow me through instead of processing them. Suppressing uncomfortable emo- tions limits our personal potential and relationship with God and others over time. It will eventually catch up with us.

05 Finding My Value in Accomplishment

One thing I am becoming more and more convinced of is that shame drives most of our existence, or perhaps at least mine. We are either living out of the freedom of who Jesus says that we are in His grace, or we are living out of shame. This side of heaven, we are never living purely in one or the other, but we can draw more and more of our iden- tity from God's grace. Shame drives us to look for value and signifi- cance somewhere other than in dependent and joyful affirmation from Jesus. One of the places I've looked for significance outside of Jesus is finding my value in accomplishments. This drives me at the deepest places if I am not aware and purposeful about reorienting to the embrace of Jesus. There is a vast difference between living to FIND value and significance and living FROM value and significance. I get these mixed up. But when I slow down, when I look at my story, and allow myself in God's grace to go to the most brutally honest places inside, then I can see it.

As I reflected on these five challenges, in the process of writing them, I can think of situations, relationships and seasons of time when I behaved in ways I regret. But I am able to also write them down with a deep sense of safety and hopefulness because God has covered me in His grace. He empowers me by His spirit and works for my good in every situation. Someday, He will finish what he started in me. Until then, I am on a journey of graceful growth, pressing on into resurrection living.

Use the space below to identify your five challenges if you know what they are. You may need more time, reflection and digging deeper into your story and emotions to develop this personal list. Write down and elaborate on the ones you know now (some could be similar to my own). For the ones you do not yet know, return to this page as you discover them.

1.

2.

3.

4.

5.

A person with a strong and true sense of identity will experience peace with self, others and God. This person will have a certain self-forgetfulness, a lack of self-absorption and self-consciousness. By contrast, the person with a weak sense of identity is painfully concerned with him or herself.

Dick Keys, Beyond Identity

FOUR SHIFTS FOR GROWTH

Doing what we've always done will get us what we've always got. Growth comes as we reflect, question and recognize in God's grace that we are still on a transformation journey. This means we must be learners, who always have their antennas up to the principles, practices and paradigms that will help us blossom emotionally. While there are whole books written on these shifts, in the space below I will highlight four.

01 Explore How Emotional Environments and Experiences of the Past are Shaping Your Present

Exploring the past opens the doors to the present. All of us carry pain and limiting patterns of coping behaviors that hold us back if they go unchecked. Our family of origin shapes us powerfully, many times in ways we do not fully see. "While there are many factors that influence this development of emotional intelligence from childhood into adolescent and into adulthood, none has as much influence as one's family of origin." [19] By exploring the healthy and unhealthy emotional patterns we saw modeled in our families, we can begin to negate the negative influences acting upon or EI and be opened up to God's healing path. When we explore the people and experiences that have shaped us significantly, we are bringing into the conscious what would otherwise remain a hidden driver of our attitude, beliefs and behaviors. This means we start with our families and move outward in our experiences, paying attention to how our story has been shaped through our journey. For most of us, as we understand how our current approaches to emotions has been shaped by the past, there will be both blessings to celebrate and challenges to process.

How has your past experiences and environments shaped you emotionally?

02 Move up the Ladder of Awareness

One of the meta-disciplines that can really fuel growth in our EI is ascending the ladder of emotional awareness. In the *Emotional Intelligence Handbook*, Richard Lane describes the levels of awareness as:

> "The five levels of emotional awareness in ascending order are physical sensations, action tendencies, single emotions, blends of emotions, and blends of blends of emotional experience (the capacity to appreciate complexity in the experiences of the self and others)." [20]

We may start by recognizing that our face is getting red or our shoulders are feeling tight, this is the most basic level of awareness. As we grow in awareness, we will realize that we have certain patterns of behavior that relate to specific triggers. An example of this next level of awareness may be that every time we come home from work, we are quick to be short with our words towards a spouse or child, or that every time we lead a meeting, we interrupt people who we disagree with. At this state of awareness, we are recognizing 'action tendencies,' and are able to observe our own behavior. The next level is recognizing that we are feeling angry or that we are feeling afraid of looking stupid in the meeting and that is driving our behavior. So in this example, we move from recognizing that our fist is clenched (physical sensations), to realizing that we are interrupting those who disagree with us (action tendencies), to realizing that we feel afraid or angry. The ladder continues with recognizing blends of emotions like fear and sadness or anger and sadness onward to complex blends of various emotions. Our physiology is triggered before we come into awareness of an emotion, but we can grow in our ability to ascend from outer physical sensations to feeling internally. We will also grow in the timing of our recognition. As we practice awareness through meditation, reflection and mindfulness throughout the day, we will slowly move from cultivating awareness after the meeting is over to awareness in the meeting, then to awareness of our emotions before the meeting. All emotional intelligence is built from our accurate awareness of self, God and others.

03 Develop Emotional Agility

In a very helpful article in Harvard Business Review, authors Susan David and Christina Congleton explore four practices to navigate negative emotional thoughts and feelings in order to cultivate emotional agility. They describe the four practices below.

- "Recognize your patterns

- Label your thoughts and emotions
- Accept them
- Act on your values" [21]

Developing emotional agility means practicing the above effective inner-strategies when we feel stuck with thoughts or emotions. By recognizing patterns, we move from passively blaming our environment to taking healthy ownership of our brokenness. If we are fired from multiple jobs for an inability to work with others, we can try blaming those we are always stuck working with, but that won't help us make the likely shifts we need to in order to have success at our next job. The authors describe how the simple act of labeling our thoughts, emotions and patterns moves us out of a captivated interpretation to a place where we can explore and examine them. Labeling moves us one step up the ladder in recognition, in being able to step back and see ourselves with greater insight. If we cannot label our emotions we are likely to be driven by them, possible into a values conflict.

The next practice is to accept them, instead of seeking to suppress or be carried away by them. We simply acknowledge them and let ourselves experience our emotions. If we refuse to acknowledge and experience them, we will not be honest with ourselves at the core level needed in order to really explore our feelings. Accepting them isn't a value judgment or approval, it simply is acknowledging what we feel. Before we can understand or respond, we must first not hide from what we are feeling. Lastly, we are invited to act on our values. We may feel strongly and can still choose to act on our values in a manner that leads to health. As a child, we may have our toy taken and we hit the aggressor. When questioned, we simply state that they took our toy, as if there are no other options. As we mature emotionally, we recognize other healthy options for dealing with hurt, loss or unhealthy behaviors by others. We learn to set boundaries and be honest in a manner that doesn't hold hurt in our lash out in anger. That is acting on values instead of simply acting on emotion. Another example of this is not exercising, a challenge I have faced. Instead of acting on the feeling that would keep me passive, I choose to act on the value of health that enables me to get on the tread-mill. We can feel anger without hurting others. We can feel sadness without turning to an affair, cutting off friends and family or pursuing an unhealthy escape. Acting on values doesn't mean ignore or suppress, but rather that we choose healthy lives from an integrated core. A core where we are fully alive emotionally and actively pursuing pathways that will lead to life in Jesus.

04 Recognize Your Typical Patterns

Daniel Goleman describes three styles for attending and dealing with emotions, and I have added a fourth. We all tend to act out one of these styles in our typical patterns of how we approach our emotional life. Here are the four:

Self-aware: Aware of their moods as they are having them, these people understandably have some sophistication about their emotional lives

Engulfed: These are people who often feel swamped by their emotions and helpless to escape them, as though their moods have taken charge

Suppression: These people are mainly unaware, not allowing them-selves to become fully aware of their emotions [my addition]

Accepting: While these people are often clear about what they are feeling, they also tend to be accepting of their moods, and so don't try to change them [22]

If our typical pattern is engulfed, processing our inner core may be helpful in discovering further healing and freedom. Identifying practical strategies for responding may also help us move towards self-awareness. Action steps for moving from suppression to self-aware might include calendaring time for self-reflection, emotional checkups. It may also include looking at the emotional chart daily included in this journal and utilizing it to help get under the surface to identify emotions. Those of us who identify with accepting will benefit from continuing to be clear about what we are feeling, but instead of resorting to passivity, we choose to actively engage. This means healthily processing our emotions and recognizing that though we cannot control them we can certainly influence them through various means like exercise, focus, friendship, reflection and reframing. The goal isn't to get rid of uncomfortable emotions, but rather to not become stuck on our journey in passivity. God grows us through healthy sadness and anger, He meets us in those places just as much as He meets us in our joy and peace.

Recognizing our typical patterns for processing our emotions is essential to growing our EI. As we understand how we have learned to experience emotions, we can purposefully choose helpful strategies to increase our EI abilities and correct limiting approaches that we have developed over time.

Use the space below to identify 2-3 shifts that would empower your growth.

FEELINGS CHART

As we seek to grow in our EI, being able to identify what we are experiencing will greatly help us in our growth. The feeling chart on the next page is a tool that we can use to help identify our emotions with greater nuance. Expanding our vocabulary isn't just an exercise in growing our intellect, it is an exercise in recognizing accurately the intensity of our feelings. Are we glad or thrilled, disappointed or depressed, irritated or furious? Developing a greater range of language will enable us to experience a greater range of emotions with self-awareness. This is essential before we can also seek to understand and respond in a life-giving manner.

As you enter into the journal, pull from this tool to help increase awareness each day.

The five core emotions run left to right across the top of the table. Manifestations of each emotion based upon the intensity felt are described down each of the columns in the table. [23]

INTENSITY OF FEELINGS	HAPPY	SAD
HIGH	Elated Excited Overjoyed Thrilled Exuberant Ecstatic Fired up Passionate	Depressed Agonized Alone Hurt Dejected Hopeless Sorrowful Miserable
MEDIUM	Cheerful Gratified Good Relieved Satisfied Glowing	Heartbroken Somber Lost Distressed Let down Melancholy
LOW	Glad Contented Pleasant Tender Pleased Mellow	Unhappy Moody Blue Upset Disappointed Dissatisfied

ANGRY	AFRAID	ASHAMED
Furious	Terrified	Sorrowful
Enraged	Horrified	Remorseful
Outraged	Scared stiff	Defamed
Boiling	Petrified	Worthless
Irate	Fearful	Disgraced
Seething	Panicky	Dishonored
Loathsome	Frantic	Mortified
Betrayed	Shocked	Admonished

Upset	Apprehensive	Apologetic
Mad	Frightened	Unworthy
Defended	Threatened	Sneaky
Frustrated	Insecure	Guilty
Agitated	Uneasy	Embarrassed
Disgusted	Intimidated	Secretive

Perturbed	Cautious	Bashful
Annoyed	Nervous	Ridiculous
Uptight	Worried	Regretful
Resistant	Timid	Uncomfortable
Irritated	Unsure	Pitied
Touchy	Anxious	Silly

2 Corinthians 5:17-21

Therefore, if anyone is in Christ, the new creation has come: The old has gone, the new is here! All this is from God, who reconciled us to himself through Christ and gave us the ministry of reconciliation: that God was reconciling the world to himself in Christ, not counting people's sins against them. And he has committed to us the message of reconciliation. We are therefore Christ's ambassadors, as though God were making his appeal through us. We implore you on Christ's behalf: Be reconciled to God. God made him who had no sin to be sin for us, so that in him we might become the righteousness of God.

DAY 1
"Change begins with a question"
Michael Pfau

Morning

How did I feel as I started the day?

How will I choose to process these emotions?

Midday

Am I aware of what I am feeling as I encounter people and situations in my day?

How am I responding to these emotions?

Evening

Was I honest with myself and others today?

What was the strongest emotion that I felt today?

What do you desire to change in yourself or your life?

Write out a prayer to the Lord that includes your emotional experience from today.

Psalm 23

The Lord is my shepherd, I lack nothing.
He makes me lie down in green pastures,
he leads me beside quiet waters,
he refreshes my soul.
He guides me along the right paths
for his name's sake.
Even though I walk
through the darkest valley,
I will fear no evil,
for you are with me;
your rod and your staff,
they comfort me.
You prepare a table before me
in the presence of my enemies.
You anoint my head with oil;
my cup overflows.
Surely your goodness and love will follow me
all the days of my life,
and I will dwell in the house of the Lord forever.

DAY 2

"When we do not process before God the very feelings that make us human,
such as fear, sadness or anger, we leak."
Peter Scazzero, Emotionally Healthy Spirituality

Reflection for morning

What did I wake up feeling today? How am I processing these emotions?

What am I thankful for?

Reflection for afternoon/evening

Was I aware of my emotions throughout the day?

What emotions am I not processing? Where am I leaking?

Did I live authentically with others today?

Write out a prayer to the Lord that includes your emotional experience from today.

Colossians 2:13-15

When you were dead in your sins and in the uncircumcision of your flesh, God made you alive with Christ. He forgave us all our sins, having canceled the charge of our legal indebtedness, which stood against us and condemned us; he has taken it away, nailing it to the cross. And having disarmed the powers and authorities, he made a public spectacle of them, triumphing over them by the cross.

DAY 3

"Without recognizing our own emotions, we will be poor at managing them, and less able to understand them in others."

Goleman, Boyatzis & McKee, Primal Leadership

Questions for reflection

What did I bring with me internally into the day?

Where am I ignoring emotions in unhealthy ways?

In what ways am I experiencing joy or sadness?

How has living unaware of my emotions hurt me, my relationships or my work environments in the past?

Write out a prayer to the Lord that includes your emotional experience from today.

1 Peter 2:9-10

But you are a chosen race, a royal priesthood, a holy nation, a people for his own possession, that you may proclaim the excellencies of him who called you out of darkness into his marvelous light. Once you were not a people, but now you are God's people; once you had not received mercy, but now you have received mercy.

DAY 4

"Emotional intelligence is your ability to recognize and understand emotions in yourself and others, and your ability to use this awareness to manage your behavior and relationships"
Travis Bradberry and Jean Gleaves, Emotional Intelligence 2.0

Morning

What emotions am I bringing into the day?

How will I choose to respond?

Midday

On a scale of 1-5, how aware are you of your emotions today?

1-confusion 2   *3*   *4*   *5-strong awareness*

On a scale of 1-5, how well did understand those emotions?

1-confusion 2   *3*   *4*   *5-strong understanding*

Did your responses to your emotions help or hurt you in living emotionally healthy today?

What was the strongest emotion that you felt today?

Write out a prayer to the Lord that includes your emotional experience from today.

Genesis 1:27

So God created mankind in his own image,

in the image of God he created them;

male and female he created them.

DAY 5

"Self-awareness is not an attention that gets carried away by emotions, overreacting and amplifying what is perceived. Rather, it is a neutral mode that maintains self-reflectiveness even amidst turbulent emotions."

Daniel Goleman, Emotional Intelligence: Why It Can Matter More Than IQ

Morning

How did I wake-up feeling today?

How will I choose to respond?

Midday

Am I aware of what I am feeling as I encounter people and situations in my day?

How am I responding to these emotions?

Evening

Was I honest with myself and others today?

What was the strongest emotion that I felt today?

Write out a prayer to the Lord that includes your emotional experience from today.

1 Peter 2:9-10

But you are a chosen race, a royal priesthood, a holy nation, a people for his own possession, that you may proclaim the excellencies of him who called you out of darkness into his marvelous light. Once you were not a people, but now you are God's people; once you had not received mercy, but now you have received mercy.

DAY 6

"Self-aware leaders are attuned to their inner signals"
Goleman, Boyatzis & McKee, Primal Leadership

Morning

How did I feel as I got up today?

What emotions have I been carrying with me this week?

Midday

Am I aware of what I am feeling as I encounter people and situations in my day?

How am I responding to these emotions?

Evening

Was I honest with myself and others today?

What was the strongest emotion that I felt today?

What emotional inner signals have you been aware of in the past?

Write out a prayer to the Lord that includes your emotional experience from today.

Psalm 119:25-28
I am laid low in the dust;
preserve my life according to your word.
I gave an account of my ways and you answered me;
teach me your decrees.
Cause me to understand the way of your precepts,
that I may meditate on your wonderful deeds.
My soul is weary with sorrow;
strengthen me according to your word.

DAY 7

"Most people are either 'stuffers' or 'inflictors' of their anger. Some are both,
stuffing until they final explode onto others."
Peter Scazzero, Emotionally Healthy Spirituality

Morning

How did I wake feeling today?

What am I thankful for?

Midday

Am I aware of what I am feeling as I encounter people and situations in my day?

How am I responding to these emotions?

Evening

Was I honest with myself and others today?

What was the strongest emotion that I felt today?

Do you tend towards stuffing or inflicting when you feel angry?

Write out a prayer to the Lord that includes your emotional experience from today.

Psalm 34:17-18

The righteous cry out, and the Lord hears them;
he delivers them from all their troubles.
The Lord is close to the brokenhearted
and saves those who are crushed in spirit.

DAY 8

"While there are many factors that influence this development of emotional intelligence from childhood into adolescent and into adulthood, none has as much influence as one's family of origin."
Bob Burns, Tasha Chapman & Donald Guthrie, Resilient Ministry

Questions for reflection

How did my family approach emotions?

How did growing up in my family shape my emotional journey?

Midday

What patterns from my family do I need keep holding onto as it relates to emotional health?

What patterns from my family do I need to let go of as it relates to emotional health?

Write out a prayer to the Lord that includes your emotional experience from today.

Mark 1:35

Very early in the morning, while it was still dark, Jesus got up, left the house and went off to a solitary place, where he prayed.

DAY 9

*"By understanding what emotional intelligence really is and how
we can manage it in our lives, we can begin to leverage all of that intelligence,
education and experience we've been storing up for all these years"*
Patrick Lencioni, Emotional Intelligence 2.0 Preface

Reflect on this quote as it interacts with your life in the space provided.

Questions for reflection

What emotions do you bring into your day?

Has your approach to your emotions helped or hurt you in your relationships, home life and work?

Write a future vision of yourself emotionally in 4-5 sentences.

Write out a prayer to the Lord that includes your emotional experience from today.

Matthew 3:16-17

And when Jesus was baptized, immediately he went up from the water, and behold, the heavens were opened to him, and he saw the Spirit of God descending like a dove and coming to rest on him; and behold, a voice from heaven said, "This is my beloved Son, with whom I am well pleased.

DAY 10

"It is important to remember that it is your own thoughts, bodily changes and behaviors that drive your emotional responses, not someone else's actions or an external event."
H. Weisinger, *Managing Your Emotions*

Questions for reflection

What emotions are you bringing into your day?

What are you grateful for?

What emotions did you experience as you look back over your day?

As you reflect, is there anything you would change in your responses?

Write out a prayer to the Lord that includes your emotional experience from today.

Psalm 22:1-5

My God, my God, why have you forsaken me?

Why are you so far from saving me,

so far from my cries of anguish?

My God, I cry out by day, but you do not answer,

by night, but I find no rest.

Yet you are enthroned as the Holy One;

you are the one Israel praises.

In you our ancestors put their trust;

they trusted and you delivered them.

To you they cried out and were saved;

in you they trusted and were not put to shame.

DAY 11

"Self-management is your ability to use your awareness of your emotions to actually choose what you say and do."
Travis Bradberry and Jean Greaves, Emotional Intelligence 2.0

Questions for reflection

How aware are you of others' emotions?

As you look back over the last week, where have you practiced empathy, the act of seeing and feeling from someone's perspective?

What might God being communicating to you today through your emotional experiences?

Write out a prayer to the Lord that includes your emotional experience from today.

Psalm 30:8-12

To you, Lord, I called;
to the Lord I cried for mercy:
"What is gained if I am silenced,
if I go down to the pit?
Will the dust praise you?
Will it proclaim your faithfulness?
Hear, Lord, and be merciful to me;
Lord, be my help."
You turned my wailing into dancing;
you removed my sackcloth and clothed me with joy,
that my heart may sing your praises and not be silent.
Lord my God, I will praise you forever.

DAY 12

"People who are upset have trouble reading emotions accurately in other people—decreasing the most basic skill needed for empathy and, as a result, impairing their social skills"
Goleman, Boyatzis & McKee, Primal Leadership

Reflect on this quote as it interacts with your life in the space provided.

Describe the emotions you felt and how you responded throughout your day

Morning

Midday

Evening

When you feel strong emotions, how do you respond to them?

Write out a prayer to the Lord that includes your emotional experience from today.

Philippians 4:4-9

Rejoice in the Lord always. I will say it again: Rejoice! Let your gentleness be evident to all. The Lord is near. Do not be anxious about anything, but in every situation, by prayer and petition, with thanksgiving, present your requests to God. And the peace of God, which transcends all understanding, will guard your hearts and your minds in Christ Jesus.

Finally, brothers and sisters, whatever is true, whatever is noble, whatever is right, whatever is pure, whatever is lovely, whatever is admirable—if anything is excellent or praiseworthy—think about such things. Whatever you have learned or received or heard from me, or seen in me—put it into practice. And the God of peace will be with you.

DAY 13

"I discovered that my life is a lot like an iceberg—I was aware of only a fraction of it and largely unaware of the hidden mass beneath the surface. And it was that hidden mass that had wreaked havoc on my family and on my leadership."

Peter Scazzero, *The Emotionally Healthy Leader*

Reflect on this quote as it interacts with your life in the space provided.

What is in your hidden mass underneath the surface of your life emotionally?

Describe the emotions you felt and how you responded throughout your day

Morning

Midday

Evening

Write out a prayer to the Lord that includes your emotional experience from today.

Colossians 3:12-14

Therefore, as God's chosen people, holy and dearly loved, clothe yourselves with compassion, kindness, humility, gentleness and patience. Bear with each other and forgive one another if any of you has a grievance against someone. Forgive as the Lord forgave you. And over all these virtues put on love, which binds them all together in perfect unity.

DAY 14

"Human emotions are part of what it means to be made in the image of God"
Bob Burns, Tasha Chapman & Donald Guthrie, Resilient Ministry

Reflect on this quote as it interacts with your life in the space provided.

Describe the emotions you felt and how you responded throughout your day

Morning

Midday

Evening

Looking back, how have you viewed emotions on your journey?

What does it look like for you to appreciate emotions as a gift from God?

Write out a prayer to the Lord that includes your emotional experience from today.

Psalm 5:1-3

Listen to my words, Lord,
consider my lament.
Hear my cry for help,
my King and my God,
for to you I pray.
In the morning, Lord, you hear my voice;
in the morning I lay my requests before you
and wait expectantly.

DAY 15

"Because people are having real, and helpful, spiritual experiences in certain areas of their lives—such as worship, prayer, Bible studies, and fellowship—they mistakenly believe they are doing fine, even if their relational life and interior world is not in order"

Peter Scazzero, Emotionally Healthy Spirituality

Reflect on this quote as it interacts with your life in the space provided.

When you look at your relational and interior life, what do you see?

Describe the emotions you felt and how you responded throughout your day

Morning

Midday

Evening

Write out a prayer to the Lord that includes your emotional experience from today.

Psalm 139:23-24

Search me, God, and know my heart;
test me and know my anxious thoughts.
See if there is any offensive way in me,
and lead me in the way everlasting.

DAY 16

"Often we do not notice our own behaviors, we have conditioned ourselves to their normalcy"
H. Weisinger, Managing Your Emotions

Reflect on this quote as it interacts with your life in the space provided.

Describe the emotions you felt and how you responded throughout your day

Morning

Midday

Evening

What unhelpful behaivors can you no longer see in yourself or have accepted as normal?

Write out a prayer to the Lord that includes your emotional experience from today.

Proverbs 20:5

The purposes of a person's heart are deep waters, but one who has insight draws them out.

DAY 17

"Yet the first and most difficult task we face as leaders is to lead ourselves. Why? Because it requires confronting parts of who we are that we prefer to neglect, forget, or deny."
Peter Scazzero, The Emotionally Healthy Leader

Reflect on this quote as it interacts with your life in the space provided.

Describe the emotions you felt and how you responded throughout your day

Morning

Midday

Evening

What does it look like for you to lead yourself in emotional intelligence?

What areas are the hardest for you to be compltely honest with yourself about as you look inward?

Write out a prayer to the Lord that includes your emotional experience from today.

2 Corinthians 1:20-22

For no matter how many promises God has made, they are "Yes" in Christ. And so through him the "Amen" is spoken by us to the glory of God. Now it is God who makes both us and you stand firm in Christ. He anointed us, set his seal of ownership on us, and put his Spirit in our hearts as a deposit, guaranteeing what is to come.

DAY 18

"When you hold to a painful feeling, rather than express it spontaneously, you begin to distort it. The longer the feeling is stored, the more distorted it tends to become."
Daniel Goleman, Emotional Intelligence: Why It can Matter More Than IQ

Reflect on this quote as it interacts with your life in the space provided.

Describe the emotions you felt and how you responded throughout your day

Morning

Midday

Evening

As you examine your heart and life, are there painful feelings you are holding onto?

How can you express painful feelings so they don't become distorted

Write out a prayer to the Lord that includes your emotional experience from today.

Matthew 4:1-4

Then Jesus was led by the Spirit into the wilderness to be tempted by the devil. After fasting forty days and forty nights, he was hungry. The tempter came to him and said, "If you are the Son of God, tell these stones to become bread."

Jesus answered, "It is written: 'Man shall not live on bread alone, but on every word that comes from the mouth of God.'"

DAY 19

"Emotions that simmer beneath the threshold of awareness can have a powerful impact on how we perceive and react, even though we have no idea they are at work."
Daniel Goleman, Emotional Intelligence: Why It Can Matter More Than IQ

Reflect on this quote as it interacts with your life in the space provided.

Describe the emotions you felt and how you responded throughout your day

Morning

Midday

Evening

What emotions have driven or are currently driving your life under the surface?

Write out a prayer to the Lord that includes your emotional experience from today

Luke 9:46-48

An argument started among the disciples as to which of them would be the greatest. Jesus, knowing their thoughts, took a little child and had him stand beside him. Then he said to them, "Whoever welcomes this little child in my name welcomes me; and whoever welcomes me welcomes the one who sent me. For it is the one who is least among you all who is the greatest."

DAY 20

"Managing your emotions means something quite different from stifling them"
H. Weisinger, Managing Your Emotions

Reflect on this quote as it interacts with your life in the space provided.

Describe the emotions you felt and how you responded throughout your day

Morning

Midday

Evening

What does the difference between stifling and managing emotions look like for you?

Is the way you are currently processing emotions leading you into health?

Write out a prayer to the Lord that includes your emotional experience from today

John 13:3-5

Jesus knew that the Father had put all things under his power, and that he had come from God and was returning to God; so he got up from the meal, took off his outer clothing, and wrapped a towel around his waist. After that, he poured water into a basin and began to wash his disciples' feet, drying them with the towel that was wrapped around him.

DAY 21

"The key to intuiting another's feelings is the ability to read nonverbal channels:
the tone of voice, gesture, facial expression, and the like"
Daniel Goleman, Emotional Intelligence: Why It Can Matter More Than IQ

Reflect on this quote as it interacts with your life in the space provided.

Describe the emotions you sensed others felt and how you responded
to them today.

How do you want others to listen to you?

How do know when you are fully present and listening well?

What would be some helpful practices for you to grow as a listener?

Write out a prayer to the Lord that includes your emotional experience from today.

Philippians 2:3-4
Do nothing out of selfish ambition or vain
conceit. Rather, in humility value others above
yourselves, not looking to your own interests but each of
you to the interests of the others.

DAY 22

*"Understanding other people involves first a deciding to switch
your attention away from yourself"*
David Walton, Emotional Intelligence: A Practical Guide

Reflect on this quote as it interacts with your life in the space provided.

Describe your emotions today and how you processed them

Describe the emotions you sensed others felt today and how you responded to them

Think of a challenging situation you're currently experiencing. Reframe your perspective to view the situation through the eyes of someone else involved. How does this influence the way you see or approach that person/situation?

Write out a prayer to the Lord that includes your emotional experience from today.

Romans 8:37-39

No, in all these things we are more than conquerors through him who loved us. For I am convinced that neither death nor life, neither angels nor demons, neither the present nor the future, nor any powers, neither height nor depth, nor anything else in all creation, will be able to separate us from the love of God that is in Christ Jesus our Lord.

DAY 23

"Those struggling with shame often view others as 'normal,' acceptable, and lovable. Yet, they see themselves as flawed, damaged and different. It becomes as natural as breathing for them to shame themselves with critical self-talk."
Cynthia Humbert, Deceived by Shame

Reflect on this quote as it interacts with your life in the space provided.

Describe the emotions you felt today and how you responded to them

Describe the emotions you sensed others felt and how you responded to them

Where are you living out of shame in your life?

Where are you living out of grace?

Write out a prayer to the Lord that includes your emotional experience from today

Psalm 46:10
He says, "Be still, and know that I am God;
I will be exalted among the nations,
I will be exalted in the earth."

DAY 24

*"Awareness of yourself inside and out is a continuous journey of peeling back
the layers of the onion and becoming more comfortable with what
is in the middle-the true essence of you"*
Daniel Goleman, Emotional Intelligence: Why It Can Matter More Than IQ

Reflect on this quote as it interacts with your life in the space provided.

Describe your emotions today and how you processed them.

Describe the emotions you sensed others felt and how you responded to them.

What is a layer you feel God is currently "peeling back?"

Are you confident in his grace and goodness in this season to peel it back?

Write out a prayer to the Lord that includes your emotional experience from today.

Romans 8:28-30

And we know that in all things God works for the good of those who love him, who have been called according to his purpose. For those God foreknew he also predestined to be conformed to the image of his Son, that he might be the firstborn among many brothers and sisters. And those he predestined, he also called; those he called, he also justified; those he justified, he also glorified.

DAY 25

"To be listened to is a striking experience—partly because it is so rare. When another person is totally with you, leaning in, interested in every word, eager to empathize, you feel known and understood. People get bigger when they know they're being listening to; they have more presence. They feel safer and more secure, as well, and they can begin to trust."
Whitworth, Kimsey-House & Sandahl, Co-Active Coaching

Reflect on this quote as it interacts with your life in the space provided.

Describe the emotions you felt and how you responded throughout your day

Morning

Midday

Evening

Do others view you as trustworthy in your home, relationships and work? How do you know?

Where do you feel most known and understood?

Write out a prayer to the Lord that includes your emotional experience from today.

Genesis 2:2-3

By the seventh day God had finished the work he had been doing; so on the seventh day he rested from all his work. Then God blessed the seventh day and made it holy, because on it he rested from all the work of creating that he had done.

DAY 26

"The fact is, we often get into all kinds of trouble by inflating our role in the drama of life. Perhaps this one of the main reasons why God creates limits. He knew that without limits, we would overreach, swell with pride, and become independent. We would get priorities all messed up, and life balance would be neglected. He would have been right. So to address that problem preemptively, He created limits. We are not infinite."
Richard Swenson, The Overload Syndrome

Reflect on this quote as it interacts with your life in the space provided.

Describe the emotions you felt today and how you processed them.

Where do you find your value and significance?

How do you think God views you?

What does it look like for you to embrace your God-given limits?

Write out a prayer to the Lord that includes your emotional experience from today.

Mark 2:17

On hearing this, Jesus said to them, "It is not the healthy who need a doctor, but the sick. I have not come to call the righteous, but sinners."

DAY 27

"We are a circumference people, with little access to the center. We live on the boundaries of our own lives...confusing edges with essence, too quickly claiming the superficial as the substance...we can remain on the circumferences of our lives for quite a long time. So long, that it starts feeling like the only 'life' available."
Richard Rohr, Everything Belongs

Reflect on this quote as it interacts with your life in the space provided.

Where did you struggle with self-control today? What emotions were you feeling then?

In what ways are you living on the edges of your life?

In what ways are you living from the center?

Write out a prayer to the Lord that includes your emotional experience from today.

Romans 8:14-17

For those who are led by the Spirit of God are the children of God. The Spirit you received does not make you slaves, so that you live in fear again; rather, the Spirit you received brought about your adoption to sonship. And by him we cry, "Abba, Father." The Spirit himself testifies with our spirit that we are God's children. Now if we are children, then we are heirs—heirs of God and co-heirs with Christ, if indeed we share in his sufferings in order that we may also share in his glory.

DAY 28

"Unmet and unclear expectations create havoc in our places of employment, classrooms, friendships, dating relationships, marriages, sports teams, families, and churches."
Peter Scazzero, *Emotionally Healthy Spirituality*

Reflect on this quote as it interacts with your life in the space provided.

Where do you feel the deepest frustration with others?

Where do you feel unmet expectations at home, in relationships or at work?

Where are you putting unclear expectations onto others?

Where do you feel unfair expectations are being place upon you? How are you responding to them?

Write out a prayer to the Lord that includes your emotional experience from today.

Psalm 32:7

You are my hiding place;
you will protect me from trouble
and surround me with songs of deliverance.

DAY 29

"When your nonverbal signals match up with the words you're saying, they increase trust, clarity, and rapport. When they don't, they generate tension, mistrust and confusion"
David Walton, Emotional Intelligence: A Practical Guide

Reflect on this quote as it interacts with your life in the space provided.

Describe your emotions today and how you processed them.

Describe the emotions you sensed others felt and how you responded to them your day.

Where did you struggle with self-control today? What emotions were you feeling then?

How do you help others feel safe in your presence? Is there anything you need to start, stop or continue doing to help others be authentic with you?

Write out a prayer to the Lord that includes your emotional experience from today.

Romans 8:1

Therefore, there is now no condemnation for those who are in Christ Jesus, because through Christ Jesus the law of the Spirit who gives life has set you free from the law of sin and death.

DAY 30

"While we often miss cues about others' emotional states, we generally pay even less attention to our emotional response to God and his response to us."
Curt Thompson, Anatomy of the Soul

Reflect on this quote as it interacts with your life in the space provided.

Are you living honestly with God each day? How do you know?

How does God meet with you in your emotional reflections and experiences?

What does it look like for you to relate to God emotionally?

How is God calling you into a deeper walk with Him each day?

Write out a prayer to the Lord that includes your emotional experience from today.

LOOKING BACK ON YOUR 30 DAY JOURNEY

As your journey through the emotional intelligence journal comes to an end, take a few moments to reflect on the ups and downs of your experience.

How did you begin the journey? What words described your emotional place?

What surprised you as you paid closer attention to your emotions and those of others?

How have you grown?

Where have you uncovered unhealth to explore further?

What habits, attitudes or practices will be important for you emotionally as you continue on your journey?

Is there anywhere you need the help of others to progress?

WHERE DO I GO FROM HERE?

Rhythms and Disciplines

Key to the way we live is the rhythms and habits we centralize along the way. For some, reflection was already a key discipline, for others, this was a beginning. As we seek to live fully alive and flourishing, what will be the practices and calendar rhythms that empowers your life? One aspect of living under Jesus well with our emotions is embracing our limits. When we continuously push past the capacity God has created us with, we ultimately will find ourselves in unhealthy emotional places. Discovering empowering rhythms and habits like meditation, Sabbath and journaling will fuel flourishing.

What does a healthy rhythm for you look like?

What will be 2-3 habits that fuel emotional health for you in the next 6 months?

Readings

Growing in emotional health and intelligence may require further reading. At the end of this journal is a short list of resources you might find helpful as you continue to explore emotional healthy living. Choose one book that seems to fit where you are, and invite a friend to join you for the ride. Read, reflect and apply the insights into your life. The danger of learning is that we apply it to everyone else but ourselves. The other danger is thinking that because we can cognitively affirm something or list it as prior knowledge, we assume that means we have allowed it to touch the innermost places of our lives. This is simply not the case. When we are reading or dialoguing, we must always assume a learning posture, believing there is a deeper level in which we can experience and practice paradigms and principles we already know. There is almost an endless supply of resources out there on emotional health and intelligence, some from a Christian worldview, some not. You will notice that most of the resources I list are not from a Christian worldview. I affirm God's truth wherever it may be found.

How will you continue to grow and learn about emotional health and intelligence?

Relationships

As we grow internally, it eventually calls us into action relationally. Perhaps as you have already been on the journey you've discovered the need for more authentic friendship or for difficult conversations with a parent, spouse or coworker. The healthier we are, the more congruent we will live with our emotions. Growing in our emotional health and intelligence is a long and winding journey. One thing is for certain, it will cause us to act differently in the way we relate to others. For some this may mean giving more of ourselves emotionally, letting others in on our joy, sadness and fear. For others it will mean setting healthy boundaries with a family member or boss. It may mean we start to express hurt that we have been letting build up for years. For others it may mean verbalizing affirmation, love and encouragement to those nearest to us.

Counseling

Counseling was essential on my journey and will likely be again someday down the road. It was hard for me to go at first because others came to me as a pastor to be counseled. I was the counselor, not the counselee. Since then I have helped many enter into counseling, sharing my own experience. Counseling is healing grace from God in that it helps us live honestly and aware with ourselves, God and others. As we journey inward and open doors we have previously refused, we eventually discover a greater freedom and wholeness. Not a perfect freedom, but a greater one this side of heaven. Who should go to counseling and who shouldn't? Impossible to say in a book like this. But if any of these describe you, think about inviting a good counselor in on your journey so you don't get stuck.

- Ongoing anger
- Resentment that is building up
- Paralyzing anxiety
- Lack of energy and enthusiasm for life
- Difficult home life, regardless of how old you are now
- Lack of joy because you never measure up
- Identifying as a workaholic
- Feeling worthless, like a failure, unworthy of love and value
- Overwhelmed by a life transition
- Experience of trauma, abuse or loss

Assessments

Sometimes it is helpful to get a baseline of where we are. There are many assessments out there, but one that is affordable and comes with a great resource is Emotional Intelligence 2.0 by Travis Bradberry and Jean Greaves. In the back of this book is a code to enter as you take an online assessment that will help you discover your strengths and weaknesses in four core competencies of emotional intelligence:

- Self-awareness
- Self-management
- Social-awareness
- Relationship-management

If you desire someone to help you process your results and develop strategies for growing each area of emotional intelligence, we offer coaching through www.multiplyleaders.co. We would love to walk beside you on your journey as you grow towards your full potential in Jesus emotionally.

My Next Steps are...

OTHER RESOURCES

Travis Bradberry and Jean Greaves. Emotional Intelligence 2.0

I love EI 2.0 because it is short, practical and comes with a free online assessment that is far cheaper when purchasing the book than simply paying for the assessment alone. Excellent and accessible resource.

Bob Burns, Tasha Chapman & Donald Gutherie, Resilient Ministry

What a gold mine of a book for ministry leaders. If you happen to be in ministry, this is a must read built upon years of practical research with a group of pastors. This is a great book for any kingdom leader, but is targeted for church leaders.

Curt Thompson, Anatomy of the Soul

A friend and professor both recommended this book at the same time. I am glad they did. Curt does an excellent job of integrating a faithful

Biblical worldview and the cutting edge learning from the emotional intelligence world. Very helpful.

Daniel Goleman. Emotional Intelligence: Why It Can Matter More Than IQ

Daniel Goleman is a genius. Although we don't share the same worldview, I have gleaned so much on my journey from his groundbreaking and extremely popular works. Though he comes from an academic perspective, his writing is accessible. If you want to dive a little deeper in the neuroscience behind emotional intelligence, grab his books. If that sounds dry and boring, buy his works and read the chapters that resonate with you. Each chapter is worth the price of any of his books.

Daniel Goleman, Richard Boyatzis & Annie McKee, Primal Leadership

I included this book because it is a powerful resource in emotional intelligence as it relates to leading others. If you are in a leadership position, you need to get this one on your reading list.

Daniel Goleman, Working with Emotional Intelligence

Work and home are two of the most challenging places to practice EI. I included this book because it focuses on how to integrate emotional intelligence into your workplace. If you feel frustrated or stuck, or if you want continue to thrive in your workplace, this is a great resource.

Kerry Patterson, Joseph Greeny, Ron McMillan & Al Switzler, Crucial Conversations

Crucial Conversations is one of those books that once read, you wonder how you lived without it. Such an insightful work on the importance of having hard conversations and practical steps to do it well.

Peter Scazzero, Emotionally Healthy Spirituality

This book was a game-changer for me. It challenged my paradigms and opened me up to the need to grow emotionally healthy. It gave me a clear call to live under the reign of Jesus in my discipleship emotionally. Very helpful work on my journey. Thankful for this book.

Peter Scazzero, The Emotionally Health Leader

I couldn't wait for this book to come out and I haven't been disappointed. Peter Scazzero has a practical and insightful style that incorporates authenticity with helpful stories. I would put both of Scazzero's books into the hands of any leader on a must read list.

David Viscott, Emotional Resilience

Insightful book on emotions, especially toxic emotions and what to do with them. Others who have read it mention how helpful it was.

Hendrie Weisinger, Emotional Intelligence at Work

I found this book to be extremely insightful, with many helpful and practical applications. The author has a great ability to say profound things in simple and memorable ways.

ABOUT THE AUTHOR

Brian is a leader, pastor, and author who is passionate about helping others unlock their leadership potential in Jesus' name. He is married to his glorious wife Katie and father to his two boys whom he deeply delights in. He is a member of the staff leadership team at a multi-site church in the St Louis area where he serves as the adult ministry and next generation director. He has a Masters in Christian Ministry and is the founder of MultiplyLeaders, a resourcing, coaching and consulting organization focused on multiplying kingdom leaders. Brian is a committed coffee drinker who is in constant pursuit of the perfect cup.

MultiplyLeaders (LLC) was founded to help you unlock your leadership potential. We are passionate about equipping kingdom leaders and organization to multiply their potential in Jesus' name through resourcing, coaching and consulting. If you are interested in further resources or in a coaching relationship, please find us at www.multiplyleaders.co for more information.

NOTES

[1] Bradberry, T. & Greaves, J., Emotional Intelligence 2.0.

[2] Lane, R. The Handbook of Emotional Intelligence, pg 173

[3] Patterson, Greeny, McMillan, Switzler, Crucial Conversations, pg 108

[4] Scazzero, P. Emotionally Healthy Spirituality, pg 74

[5] Thompson, C. Anatomy of the Soul, pg 164

[6] Walton, D. Emotional Intelligence: A Practical Guide, pg 33

[7] Goleman, D. Emotional Intelligence, pg. 55

[8] Goleman, Boyatzis & McKee, Primal Leadership, pg 30, "Self-aware leaders are attuned to their inner signals"

[9] Goleman, D. Emotional Intelligence, pg 47

[10] Goleman, Boyatzis & McKee. Primal Leadership, pg 30

[11] Goleman, Boyatzis & McKee. Primal Leadership, pg. 30. "Leaders who lack this emotional self-awareness, on the other hand, might lose their temper but have no understanding of why their emotions pushed them around."

[12] Weisinger, H. Managing Your Emotions, pg 45

[13] Goleman, D. Emotional Intelligence, pg 96

[14] Smalley, G. The DNA of Relationships

[15] Goleman, D. Emotional Intelligence, pg 96

[16] Thompson, C. Anatomy of the Soul, pg, 116

[17] Walton, D. Emotional Intelligence: A Practical Guide, g. 97

[18] Patterson, Greeny, McMillan & Switzler, Crucial Conversations, 2013.

[19] Resilient Ministry, pg 105

[20] Lane, R. Emotional Intelligence Handbook, pg 173

[21] David, S. & Congleton, C. Harvard Business Review, Emotional Ability pg 91

[22] Goleman, Daniel, Emotional Intelligence 2.0, pg 48

[23] Image reproduced from http://imaginationsoup.net/2015/07/emotional-intelligence-activities-kids/

Made in the USA
San Bernardino, CA
26 September 2015